Mastering the Art:
A Step-by-Step Guide to Writing a Quality Staff Report

Chris,
Blessings!
Tamara

Tamara S. Letourneau

DEDICATION

This book is dedicated to my family. First, the president of my fan club – my husband Paul. Thank you for always supporting me and being my biggest cheerleader. I love you with all my heart! Also, to my beautiful daughters Izabel and Jade – thank you for allowing me to be your mommy. There is no greater joy than this.

CONTENTS

ACKNOWLEDGMENTS

To laugh often and much; To win the respect of intelligent people and the affection of children..; To leave the world a bit better..; To know even one life has breathed easier because you have lived. This is to have succeeded.

~ Ralph Waldo Emerson

The quote from Ralph Waldo Emerson has become my motto in life, and captures the passion I have for my career. I was 18 years old when I decided to pursue a career in local government. Since that time, it has been a dream come true to serve these communities in every capacity.

Alongside the decision to pursue this career direction, I also became interested in teaching local government – practical and reality-based local government. My classroom forum has since been one where students hear real-life stories about how to lead and make positive change in community. I am forever grateful to the universities of Cal Poly Pomona and the University of La Verne for providing me the opportunity to teach what I love.

Although my passion and dedication for my career runs deep, the most important role in my life is being my husband's wife and my children's mother.

Paul, you encouraged me to write this book and have always supported my dreams as well as the changes this career has brought to our lives. Thank you for your love and support. None of this would be possible without you. I love you with all my heart!

Izabel and Jade, nothing is more precious than being your mother. Thank you for understanding when I sometimes must work on the weekends and why I have to be gone on Tuesday nights for city council meetings. I love you both forever and always!

Thank you to all my local government friends and colleagues. Your support and friendship means the world to me. I deeply appreciate all the city managers with whom I have worked over the years for teaching me about good government and how to be the best local government leader.

A special thanks to my dear friend and colleague Alex McIntyre, City Manager of Menlo Park. He was the Assistant City Manager for the City of Arcadia when I began my local government career as an intern. Thank you for your patience in teaching me how to write a local government staff report. I am grateful for the compassion and guidance that you offered back then, and am happy to call you a lifelong friend.

To my parents, thank you for listening to me when I told you that I wanted to become a city manager, and for supporting that decision. You have attended countless ribbon cuttings, parades, groundbreaking ceremonies, and have always become a part of the communities for which I have worked. Thank you for being there to support me no matter what. I love you.

Forward

I retired in December 2011, after 40 years in local government public service. Over the course of my career, I served in four California cities, three as city manager. Like many in municipal service, I started as an intern and served in a range of positions from staff support to operational management. For the last 30 years, I served as City Manager. In this role, I managed municipal organizations as small as 150 employees with budgets in the tens of millions of dollars and as large as 1,800 employees with a budget in the hundreds of millions of dollars.

I've worked in cities where the city council meets twice monthly and where they meet weekly. The latter feels like being on an endless fast-moving treadmill where the process of preparing and reviewing staff reports and preparing to make presentations to the city council becomes a constant driving force.

As City Manager, at times it was challenging

to support staff in performing "completed staff work" and to effectively and professionally communicate the results of their efforts to the council. As Tammy points out in *Mastering the Art: A Step-by-Step Guide to Writing a Quality Staff Report for Local Government*, being able to write a staff report is not the same as being able to write an *effective* staff report. Staff who can perform completed work, write effective reports, and deliver informative presentations are essential to the efficient functioning of an organization.

I first met Tammy many years before she decided to enter local government public service—she was 12 or 13 years old. My wife and I had moved to Monrovia, California in 1977 when I accepted a position as Assistant City Manager to work for an individual I believe is one of the finest public service managers anywhere, Robert R. "Bud" Ovrom. Bud had just been appointed to his first city manager position in that Southern California town of 36,000 people and needed an assistant. I was an MPA student at the University of Southern California and needed a job. I met Tammy's parents through the local church and we've been close friends ever since. I have been privileged to cheer Tammy on as she has grown and developed as a successful local government management professional. I take pride in the fact that I may have contributed to the spark that caused her to enter the public service.

As a teenager, Tammy was always serious and mature beyond her years, which is why my wife and I often asked her to sit for our two young sons. It is not surprising to those who know Tammy that she set her sights on a career early and went about taking all the necessary steps to be successful. In addition to building an impressive resume of experience at all levels of the municipal government organization throughout her almost three decades of service, Tammy has constantly sought to learn and strengthen her own professional skills and has prioritized developing staff as well as the organization. She has also been committed to helping aspiring professionals through her teaching, writings, and conference lectures.

This book is another effort by Tammy to share her experiences and abilities to help others become more effective professionals. It is a must-have for your organizational development program. Following her own "Tammy's Tips" for writing a staff report, this book is concise and full of specific and useful tips.

Although this book is geared toward helping the staff directly performing the analysis, report preparation, and presentation, I highly recommend it to those in supervisory, management and executive positions as well. I have heard from managers on many occasions who are wrestling with the challenge of supporting their staff to write quality staff reports in a timely fashion that keeps the agenda process moving forward. Following the tips and strategies in this book will support the development of more effective and credible staff, which will also make the executive's life a lot easier.

James E. Starbird, City Manager (Retired.)

Introduction

Every great dream begins with a dreamer. Always remember, you have within you the strength, the patience, and the passion to reach for the stars to change the world.

~ Harriet Tubman

In local government, we communicate using staff reports with legislative bodies – county board of supervisors or city council. A staff report provides the background, analysis, fiscal review, and legal summary of the issue for which the legislative body then makes a decision.

Staff reports are written on a wide variety of matters, ranging from simple to complex. Simple items may include changing the date of a regular council meeting, while complex matters could involve issues such as the construction of a new shopping center in a community.

As students, we develop skills writing lengthy term papers, and become adept at properly listing references and footnotes. We get credit for lengthy explanations and complex analysis. This writing style becomes second nature to us in our academic world.

We then graduate and land our first job in local government as an intern or a management aide and our boss asks us to write our first staff report for an upcoming meeting of the legislative body. We approach this task using the familiar term-paper format. Much to our surprise, what we learned in school no longer applies. Panic sets in so we scramble to review past staff reports to learn how to complete this task rapidly.

The scenario above happened to me many years ago. I still remember all the red pen marks in the first staff report that I submitted. Fortunately, my boss saw this as a learning opportunity, and took the time to teach me the art of writing a great staff report.

Over my 29 years in local government, I have written thousands of staff reports, and have provided guidance and feedback on many others as new employees have come on board. I have also taught this skill for over 16 years in a local government course to university-level students. It is through these experiences that I recognized the need to create a helpful resource for writing a great staff report.

Mastering the Art: The Step-by-Step Guide to Writing a Quality Staff Report for Local Government will provide you with the practical information you need to learn the art of this important skill. This guide includes 11 chapters that provide step-by-step information for writing a quality staff report from beginning to end.

Local Government Agenda Packet Preparation Process

Before anything else, preparation is the key to success.

~ Alexander Graham Bell

In local government, there is a very specific process required to prepare the agenda packet for the legislative body. In most counties and cities, this is the responsibility of the county clerk's office or the city clerk's office. In smaller cities and towns, the process is completed by the city manager's office.

Regardless of how often the legislative body meets – weekly or every two weeks, the process to assemble the agenda packet for the legislative body takes several weeks to prepare, and advanced planning is required.

Planning the agenda – including order of items – is done by the city clerk, city or county manager in conjunction with the mayor. Once it is determined which agenda item or topic will be discussed by the legislative body, the staff member responsible for that item needs to prepare a report for the legislative body to be included in the agenda packet. This report is called a staff report.

The purpose of the staff report is to provide the legislative body and the public with all the information and options related to an item, so an informed decision can be made. Writing a report that is succinct, informative and thorough takes practice.

Depending on the complexity of the topic, it is important to begin writing the staff report several weeks in advance of the legislative body's meeting. This allows for the appropriate parties to review and sign the report, and ensures that the clerk's office has time to prepare the report for the agenda packet. However, there are times when that is not possible and you only have a few days to complete a staff report. Those quick turnaround deadlines are another reason why *mastering the art* of this process is critical.

Doing your homework is critical. In local government, staff need to become experts on topics quickly, and knowing where to find resources is key. Staff should then be able synthesize and translate this information into a clear and concise report for the legislative body. Generally, a staff report should be no more than three pages. There are times when five pages are necessary for topics such as environmental impact reports or development project.

Agenda/agenda packet preparation process:

- Confirm the agenda date when the topic will be discussed by the legislative body.
- Prepare the staff report well in advance of the agenda publication date.
- Obtain the appropriate approvals and signatures on the report.
- If required, make changes to the report.
- Finalize the report.
- Make the necessary copies for the county/city clerk's office.

Following the report's completion, be prepared to make a presentation and answer questions on its content to the legislative body. Each organization has different requirements related to who delivers the presentation, but the author should always be prepared to answer questions related to the staff report. In some cases, that means preparing a PowerPoint presentation and even practicing presenting the report prior to the meeting. Preparing ahead of time for the presentation of the staff report will be worth the investment of time.

Tammy's Tips
Agenda Packet Preparation Process

- Do your homework on the topic and write a thorough yet succinct report.
- Start preparing your report well in advance of the deadline to allow time to obtain the appropriate approvals
- Be prepared to make a presentation and/or answer questions on you staff report at the meeting of the legislative body.

Key Elements of a Staff Report

You have to learn the rules of the game. And then you have to play better than anyone else.

~ Albert Einstein

One of the most significant tasks we have as local government professionals is to thoroughly research an issue and write a staff report that describes the pros, cons and alternatives in an articulate and concise manner. It is not uncommon for this task to have a very tight deadline attached. This is one of the reasons why it is so vital to master the art of staff report writing in an efficient and effective manner.

Imagine the following scenario: You are a Management Analyst in the City Manager's office and your boss walks into your office one morning and asks you to write a staff report about the contract for playground equipment. You have two weeks to complete the project.

This means that the staff report must be

written, reviewed, signed by all necessary parties, and copied for the agenda packets to be distributed to the council and the legislative body for the next city council meeting.

Before you begin making phone calls and conducting the research for the report, it is essential to sketch out the outline. Ensure that you confirm your agency's exact format and specific requirements for staff reports. Although requirements may vary slightly across agencies, the majority of local government agencies require staff reports to follow the order below in some form:

- Recommendation
- Background
- Analysis
- Alternatives
- Fiscal Review
- Legal Review
- Conclusion

If the staff report is regarding a planning project or public works project an "environment review" section may be required. The city attorney's office will make that determination if this is necessary. If it is, it should come after the "Analysis" section. The details regarding what needs to be included in each section will be described in the chapters that follow.

Tammy's Tips
Key Elements of a Staff Report

- Determine the agenda report format for your agency
- Plan ahead.
- Do your research.

Recommendation

Our goals can only be reached through a vehicle of a plan in which we must fervently believe, and upon which we must vigorously act. There is no other route to success.

~ Pablo Picasso

Now, I know what you are thinking: "Why is Chapter 3 about the recommendation when I haven't yet written the staff report? This must be a mistake." No, it is not a mistake. When an agenda packet is prepared for the legislative body, it contains at least a dozen staff reports, and can be four to five inches thick. An elected official usually only has a few days to read all the reports prior to the meeting, which means many hours of reading that is required on very complex topics.

A recommendation is included as the first section of the staff report to provide the elected official and the public with three or four sentences summarizing the issue, along with the staff recommendation. After reading a properly-written recommendation, the reader should have a clear understanding for the issue and of the recommendation put forward for approval by staff.

The following is an example of a properly-written recommendation:

> *Staff recommends that the City Council approve the contract with Play Equipment USA in the amount not to exceed $156,727 for the playground equipment in Grace Park. Further, staff recommends that the City Council direct the City Manager to sign the agreement.*

There are a few key points to remember when writing a recommendation. The first is to be very specific, and secondly to ensure that the recommendation is no more than three or four sentences.

The recommendation should start with "*Staff recommends that* (add name of the legislative body – city council, supervisors or board)..." and then add your specific recommendation(s). In some cases, there may be multiple recommendations. For example, for the approval of a development project the recommendation may read as follows:

Staff recommends that the City Council approve the following for the project at 123

Lemon Street:

1. Certify the Environmental Impact Report (EIR);
2. Approve the Zone Change;
3. Approve the Development Agreement; and,
4. Approve a Tentative Track Map

Tammy's Tips
Recommendation

- Ensure your staff recommendation is brief.
- Keep it short. The rationale for the recommendation will be explained later in the report.

Background

Don't wait. The time will never be just right.

~ Napoleon Hill

Now that you have completed your recommendation, it is time to describe the issue in the background section. In this section, you need to begin to tell the story by answering the following questions:

- Where did the issue begin?
- What occurred between the beginning and present-day requiring the legislative body to make a decision?

The following is an example of a background section utilizing the playground equipment issue:

The current playground equipment in Grace Park was installed in 1985. Numerous repairs have been made to keep the equipment in good condition, but it is past its useful life.

For the last year, the City has

received 24 complaints from residents and visitors about the poor condition of the playground equipment at Grace Park.

In the 2016, City Council goal-setting session, the City Council set the upgrade of playground equipment in Grace Park as a top-tier priority.

In the background section, it is important to be specific. If there was a city council meeting in which the issue was discussed previously or a vote was taken as part of this issue state the specific meeting in which that took place. If there were complaints received about an issue, state how many. It is vital for the legislative body and the public to understand the magnitude of the issue. The background section provides perspective and sets the tone for the section to follow, the analysis.

Tammy's Tips
Background

- Tell the story of how the issue began.
- Be specific. State dates of meetings, number of complaints, etc.

Analysis

Doing your best at this moment puts you in the best place for the next moment.

~ Oprah Winfrey

The analysis section is where you share the 'heart' of the story. Here, you provide a thorough explanation of the issue – from beginning to end.

As you write the analysis, provide the legislative body with all the information they need to make an informed decision. Some of the questions you may respond to include: Were community consultations or meetings held? Was a community survey conducted? If so, what were the results? Ensure the findings are presented in a clear, easy-to-understand format. Use tables and charts to illustrate key points, as needed.

The art of this section is providing all relevant information while being succinct. The analysis points to the reasons for the staff recommendation, which then lead to the conclusion. List the pros and cons of the staff recommendation and state why staff believes this is the best approach on the issue.

Tammy's Tips
Analysis

- Make the analysis the "heart" of the story.
- Be thorough but succinct.
- State the staff recommendation.
- Provide the pros and cons of the staff recommendation.

Fiscal Review

The cold harsh reality is that we have to balance the budget.

~ Michael Bloomberg

The fiscal analysis of the staff report is critical. In this section, it is important to fully explain the costs of the recommendation as well as alternative options. Charts, tables and other visual representations can be helpful to clearly demonstrate the total costs and/or savings to the organization.

Further, it is necessary to share the account source for the funding or where savings will be achieved with the legislative body. In local government within the United States, our discretionary funding source is called the 'General Fund'. There are also special funds – Gas Tax, Vehicles Replacement Funds, Water Funds, etc. The legislative body must be provided with this information before they make a decision. The key is to be thorough in your fiscal analysis and clearly explain the financial implications of the action for which you are asking the legislative body.

There are instances where there is no fiscal

impact on an item. An example may be where city council is designating one council member to vote on a regional committee. However, in this scenario, it is still necessary to include this information. The text in the fiscal review section should read "*There is no fiscal impact as a result of this action.*"

Tammy's Tips
Fiscal Review

- Provide a thorough analysis of the costs and/or savings.
- State the fund(s) that are impacted by this action.
- If there is no fiscal impact, be sure to include this in the staff report.

Legal Review

*Change is the law of life. And those
who look only to the past or present
are certain to miss the future.*

~ John F. Kennedy

A legal review by the city attorney or legal
counsel may be necessary, depending on the
subject of the staff report. Even if the staff
report does not require a legal review, the
section should still be included in the report,
to read *"No legal review is required for this
report."*

However, the majority of reports will require
some type of legal review, which should be
factored into your timeline. It can take at
least a day for this analysis to be completed
depending on the complexity of the topic.

If the item is a simple review of a policy or
resolution, the city or county attorney will
approve it, and give you permission to write
the following into the staff report, *"The City
Attorney (or County Counsel) has approved
this as to form."* There will be a signature
line at the end of the report confirming their
approval of this statement. If a lengthy legal

analysis is required due to the complex nature of the topic, you should work with the city attorney or county counsel on the appropriate language for this section.

Tammy's Tips
Legal Review

- Determine if a legal review is needed.
- Ensure the city/county attorney's comments are included in the report.

Alternatives

When you have two alternatives,
the first thing you have to do is to
look for the third that you didn't
think about, that doesn't exist.

~ Shimon Peres

As government professionals, our job is to honestly and thoroughly lay out all the possible alternatives on each issue. This includes accurately describing the pros and cons for the legislative body to consider.

While I have seen staff write "*none*" in the alternatives section, this is not accurate. There are always alternatives, even if the alternative is to deny the action. The denial of that action has a consequence, which needs to be described.

An example of a properly-written alternative is as follows:

1. The City Council can decide not to approve the contract with Play Equipment USA and leave the park land open space.

5. The City Council can direct staff to reject the bids and redesign the park. This would require a new RFP process and will delay the park improvements for at least 12 months.

It is necessary to thoroughly analyze all alternatives and state the consequences of such actions as objectively as possible. Although staff may prefer that the legislative body does not select the alternatives, this body has been elected by the people to make the best informed decisions. The role of staff is to thoroughly research the item and present the facts.

Tammy's Tips
Alternatives

- State all possible alternatives in the staff report, including the option to do nothing.
- State the facts and keep emotion out of the statements.

Conclusion

In a moment of decision, the best thing you can do is the right thing to do, the next best thing is the wrong thing, and the worst thing you can do is nothing.

~ Theodore Roosevelt

The conclusion is where you pull everything together. It is only a few sentences, but has a powerful impact.

This section includes the summary of the issue, a statement of why it is important, and a restatement of the recommendation. It should focus on highlighting the importance of taking the action you are proposing to the legislative body.

In the conclusion, you will restate both the summary of the issue as well as the recommendation. This is important because someone taking only a brief glance at the recommendation and conclusion sections should be able to clearly understand the issue as well as the recommendation to the legislative body.

Continuing with the playground equipment example from previous chapters, the following is a properly-written conclusion:

The new playground in Grace Park will provide a wonderful new area for children to play and families to gather. Staff recommends that the City Council approve the agreement with Play Equipment USA in the amount of $156,727.

Tammy's Tips
Conclusion

- Keep the conclusion brief — a few sentences.
- Summarize the issue.
- State why the action is important.
- Restate the staff recommendation.

Finishing the Process

It always seems impossible until it's done.

~ Nelson Mandela

Congratulations! You have completed the staff report. Now it is time to finish the process. This includes making sure all of the attachments are included with the staff report. In some cases, there are no attachments. It all depends on the type of staff report it is. In the example regarding playground equipment, the attachments are the proposed agreement between the city and the playground equipment company and the request for proposal. For a development project, there would be site plans and maps.

Next, obtain the signatures of those who need to sign the report. You should sign the report as well as your supervisor. Every organization has different requirements for who signs staff reports. Sometimes it can include your supervisor, city attorney, finance director and/or city manager. Find out what the process is in your agency.

After you have all of the attachments and

signatures follow the process established by the clerk's office regarding making copies for the legislative body and the public as well as uploading the completed report to an agenda software system (if required).

Now that the staff report is complete it is time to start preparing to present your staff report to the legislative body. Depending upon the complexity of the report and the level of interest in the issue a formal presentation will be required. This may mean preparing a PowerPoint presentation as well.

At the very least be sure to practice your presentation and being ready to answer questions. Set aside a little time to practice your presentation with your supervisor and/or a few colleagues to help refine your presentation and your comfort level with the material. The more you practice the better you will become in presenting the material.

Tammy's Tips
Finishing the Process

- Include all necessary attachments.
- Obtain signatures on the staff report.
- Prepare for the presentation.
- Practice the presentation.

Tammy's Tips

It is the supreme art of the teacher to awaken joy in creative expression and knowledge.

~ Albert Einstein

Agenda Packet Process

- Do your homework on the topic and be thorough while keeping the report brief.
- Start preparing your report well in advance of the deadline to allow time to obtain the appropriate approvals.
- Be prepared to answer questions and make a presentation on your report.

Key Elements of a Staff Report

- Determine the agenda report format for your agency.
- Plan ahead.
- Do your research.

Recommendation

- Ensure your staff recommendation is brief.
- Keep it short. The rationale for the recommendation will be explained later in the report.

Background

- Tell the story of how the issue began.
- Be specific – state dates of meetings, number of complaints, etc.

Analysis

- Make the analysis the 'heart' of the story.
- Be thorough, but succinct.
- State the staff recommendation.
- Provide the pros and cons of the staff recommendation.

Fiscal Review

- Provide a thorough analysis of the costs and/or savings.
- State the fund(s) that are impacted by this action.
- If there is no fiscal impact, be sure to include this in the staff report.

Legal Review

- Determine if a legal review is needed.
- Ensure the city/county attorney's comments are included in the report.

Alternatives

- State all possible alternatives in the staff report, including the option to do nothing.
- State the facts and keep the emotion out of the statements.

Conclusion

- Keep the conclusion brief – a few sentences.
- Summarize the issue.
- State why the action is important.
- Restate the staff recommendation.

Finishing the Process

- Include all necessary attachments.
- Obtain signatures on the staff report.
- Prepare for the presentation.
- Practice the presentation.

Appendix

Sample Staff Report Format

City of Happiness
Staff Report

TO: City Council

FROM: Tamara S. Letourneau, City
                Manager

DATE: August 1, 2017

SUBJECT: GRACE PARK
                PLAYGROUND
                EQUIPMENT CONTRACT

Recommendation

Staff recommends that the City Council
approve the agreement (Attachment 1) with
Play Equipment USA in the amount not to
exceed $156,727 for the playground
equipment in Grace Park. Further, staff
recommends that the City Council direct the
City Manager to sign the agreement.

Background

The current playground equipment in Grace Park was installed in 1985. Numerous repairs have been made to keep the equipment in good condition, but it is past its useful life.

For the last year, the City has received 24 complaints from residents and visitors about the poor condition of the playground equipment at Grace Park.

In the 2016 City Council goal-setting session, the City Council set the upgrade of playground equipment in Grace Park as a top tier priority.

Analysis

In January, the City Council directed staff to begin the process of assessing the current playground equipment and options for various designs. Staff developed three possible designs and held a neighborhood meeting in March 2017 to obtain feedback on the three options.

At the neighborhood meeting, there were 127 neighbors in attendance. They overwhelmingly favored Option #2, which includes swings, slides and monkey bars, as well as a castle with a climbing wall.

Following the neighborhood meeting, staff sent out an electronic survey seeking feedback on the three playground equipment options to those who could not attend the meeting in person. The results of the community survey and the neighborhood meeting are listed in the table below.

Park Plan Options	Neighborhood Meeting	Electronic Survey
Option 1	32	1,086
Option 2	82	2,247
Option 3	9	592
None	4	448

The table shows that in the neighborhood meeting and the electronic survey, Option 2 was preferred.

Option 2 will be a wonderful amenity for the community and will be an enhancement to the neighborhood. This addresses the City Council's goal of neighborhood beautification.

Staff prepared a Request for Proposal (RFP) (Attachment 2) for Option #2 for Grace Park. The City received 3 qualified bids. The lowest responsible bidder was Play Equipment USA in the amount of $156,727. Staff has reviewed the bid and checked all references for this company. Thus, staff recommends that the City Council approve the contract with Play Equipment USA in the amount not to exceed $156,727 for the playground equipment in Grace Park. Further, staff recommends that the City Council direct the City Manager to sign the agreement.

Alternatives

1. The City Council can decide not to approve the contract with Play Equipment USA and leave the park land open space.
2. The City Council can direct staff to reject the bids and redesign the park. This would require a new RFP process and will delay the park improvements for at least 12 months.

Fiscal Review

For the last two years, the City has set aside funds in the park development fund to pay for park enhancements throughout the community. There is a fund balance in this account of $750,000. Thus, funds are available in this account to pay for the $156,727 for this project. When this project is completed, there will be $593,273 remaining in the account to fund other park improvements planned throughout the City.

Legal Review

The City Attorney reviewed the agreement and approved it as to form.

Conclusion

The new playground in Grace Park will provide a wonderful new area for children to play and families to gather.

Staff recommends that the City Council approve the agreement with Play Equipment USA in the amount not to exceed $156,727 for the playground equipment in Grace Park. Further, staff recommends that the City Council direct the City Manager to sign the agreement.

_____   _____
   (Your Name)   (Your Supervisor)

_____   _____
 (Finance Director)   (City Attorney)

_____
  (City Manager)

Attachments:

1. Agreement between the City of Happiness and Play Equipment USA
2. Request for Proposal

About the Author

Tamara Letourneau is the Assistant City Manager of the City of Costa Mesa. She has over 29 years of extensive local government experience in six communities, including serving as a City Manager in Yorba Linda and Sierra Madre, California. She also served the cities of Claremont, Arcadia, and Monrovia, California in a variety of positions with increasing responsibilities.

She has a range of experience in organizational development, team building, and strategic planning. Her functional expertise includes operating and capital budgeting, human resources/risk management, labor relations, and intergovernmental relations. Most recently, she was a Senior Manager with the Management Partners consulting firm prior to joining the City of Costa Mesa in early 2014.

Tamara is an adjunct professor at California State Polytechnic University Pomona and the University of La Verne, and has been a speaker at numerous workshops and conferences about local government issues. She is also the Co-Chair of the California Consortium of the International City/County Management Association (Cal-ICMA) Ethics

Committee.

Tamara is a founding member and current board member of Women Leading Government and the League of Women in Government. In 1999, Tamara received the J. Michael Dutton Award from the Municipal Management Assistants of Southern California for her contribution to local government.

She is the author of the article "The First 100 Days – A Checklist for the First 100 Days as a New City Manager," which appeared in the May 2006 issue of *Public Management* magazine. She is also a contributor to the book *Democracy at the Doorstep, Too!* by Mike Conduff and Melissa Byrne Vossmer.

Tamara graduated from California State Polytechnic University at Pomona with a bachelor's degree in business administration and a minor in public administration. She also holds a master's degree in public administration from California State University Long Beach.

Author contact information: tsletourneau@gmail.com

Professional Endorsements

When I met young Tammy (Gates) Letourneau, she was ambitious, bright and highly interested in learning and professionally improving her skills. Knowing that I might have had a small part in helping her develop this thorough, yet simple, tool to crafting staff reports is an honor. Remembering her straightforward instruction can make anyone a better policy communicator.

Alex D. McIntyre
City Manager
City of Menlo Park

Finally, a comprehensive tool for this important aspect of government work. As a career coach for managers and aspiring managers I have struggled with the lack of resources for improving and development quality staff reports.

Mike Messina
Chief of Police (retired)
President & CEO
Messina and Associates, Inc.

As a former Yorba Linda City Councilmember and Mayor, I found Tammy's method for preparing a staff report extremely simple to follow. It was exactly the format I looked for when reading my agenda packet. Tammy's step-by-step guide is a must have for anyone who may be required to prepare a staff report.

Allan Castellano
Former Yorba Linda City Councilmember &
Mayor

This booklet needs to be in the top drawer of every new entry level analyst or assistant. I wish I had access to this when I started my career 46 years ago. As a former city manager (retired), I can attest to the fact that poorly written staff reports and not being prepared to present or answer question about it does a disservice to the elected body and the public as they try to understand the issue.

What is outlined in this booklet is exactly what a city manager expects in a city council staff report. Brevity, conciseness and clear understandable writing is the key to the city staff team looking professional. Remember the audience is not always technically knowledgeable and non-technical, non-bureaucratic language is essential. Using this booklet is what will make you a great staff report writer.

William R. (Bill) Kelly
City Manager (retired) City of Arcadia

President/CEO
Kelly Associates Management Group

Finally, a practical guide for staff in writing reports on matters going before a local government policy body. Ms. Letourneau provides step-by-step instructions for staff in conducting analysis, explaining the recommendation, options considered, cost involved, and why the issue is important for the governing body to consider it. Every local government staff person who is responsible for writing reports to present to a governing body should use this guide.

Jan Perkins
City Manager (retired)
Senior Partner, Management Partners

Made in the USA
Middletown, DE
10 July 2022

68793713R00035